baao

baao

barker associates
architecture office

ORO
EDITIONS

INTRODUCTION

An assembly is a fitted-together set of components. In this collection of projects, assemblies of elements, surfaces, and uses allow spaces to perform in multivalent ways. These assemblies inscribe records of relationships between occupants and modes of inhabitation into the built environment.

The interiors of the residential projects try to strike a balance between trace-inscribing, dense assemblies of elements, spaces, and apertures directing views outward and channeling light inward. Assemblies of circulatory elements, such as stairs and hallways, places of storage and display, built-in furniture, and furniture-scaled recesses perform the pragmatic function of maximizing the use of space. On another level, however, the dense combination of diverse uses into a single space produces an interlacing of independent spatial qualities not unlike the qualities associated with the contemporary urban environment. In any given urban space, for example, there might be groups of people walking or biking along a sidewalk, streaming past someone sitting alone reading on an open bench. That bench may be adjacent to a street-front alcove where someone monitors the counter of a newsstand.

Within retail and office interiors, assemblies of mixed programs allow spaces to serve needs that change from hour to hour and provide services to a broad range of constituencies sharing the same building infrastructure. Perimeter spaces are fixed and closed off while central spaces are open and filled with furniture on wheels. Wet zones on one side contrast with hot zones on the other. Extroverted spaces face walls of glass while introverted spaces receive only indirect light.

Strategies of nesting and layering assembled elements also allow spaces to accommodate differing scales of habitation. The careful placement of apertures in a surface can couple privacy for children with visual access needed for adult supervision. In other cases, the overlapping of assembled spaces allows for a blurring of the boundaries between private and public zones to create a sense of community. Large sliding doors erase delineations between classrooms. A shared sink basin connects users on opposite sides of a wall. In a multi-unit residential building for three generations of a single family, interior windows and shared kitchens reinforce family ties.

In other projects, assemblies of elements at threshold conditions create productive transitional zones that blur the boundaries between interior and exterior, public and private. Projecting roof overhangs and recessed doors and windows thicken the space of entry. Covered exterior spaces create pockets of semiprivate space within the otherwise public corridor of the urban street. Doors rotate away from the street to expand the path of entry and protect the interior from exposure.

In waterfront environments, threshold assemblies pierce straight through building volumes to connect entries to distant views. Assemblies of window walls and roof overhangs align to create diagonal sightlines that extend the sense of the physical space well beyond what has been built. In other instances, the orientations of windows and roof pitches diverge in order to create a tension between viewing angles that expands the perceived size of a compact space.

At the infrastructural level assemblies that propose the layering and weaving of urban-scaled facilities and systems into the elements of the urban fabric they serve stand in contrast to the modern practice of segregating services. Trains run right under offices and housing. Carpets of outdoor spaces span the distances between housing blocks and cap the train station below. Bike and pedestrian routes stitch the two levels together. In an energy-generating solar collector field adjacent to a bird sanctuary, the collectors rotate to allow visitors to observe the birds discreetly. These assemblies map diverse modes of inhabitation into the built environment across scales and contexts.

ORIGINS AND INFLUENCES

Do you come from a family of architects?

In my family there are lots of artists, engineers, and doctors—but even those who became doctors, like my parents, had an interest in the arts. My great-grandfather, Bennett Beckham Cardwell, whom I knew as a small child, was an architect. After studying at what was then called Carnegie Tech, he practiced in Lynchburg, Virginia. He won the Rome Prize in 1917, and took my great-grandmother with him from Lynchburg to Rome. He was trained in the Beaux-Arts style, and created several giant watercolors that are still in the family. He designed and built the house in which he raised my grandmother and her three brothers.

That house was notable for the fact that there was a master suite on the first floor, which was pretty unusual for its time. It had a grand stair with a generous landing that had a beautiful view of the surrounding lawn. I had general familiarity with the houses and churches in Lynchburg from his pre-Depression partnership with Samuel Craighill. His later residential work was built on property that was originally owned by my great-grandmother's family. My grandmother's three brothers lived in some of the houses across the street and down the road.

Where did you grow up?

I grew up in a suburb close to DC, so I went to the Smithsonian quite often. I remember getting excited about IM Pei's East Wing of the National Gallery when it was new. The clean geometry and angular volumes were amazing in that they translated pure geometric form into inhabitable space. The way that it connected to the West Building—through a tunnel with a waterfall—was a memorable detail. I liked going to the Hirshhorn Museum, by Gordon Bunshaft, because it, too, was spatially interesting. Once I visited other cities, like New York or Boston, I remember thinking that DC was not the most exciting place architecturally, with its uniformity of scale and materials, at least in the public buildings. Although Lafayette's planning created beautiful diagonal vistas, which cut through the urban landscape, restrictions on building construction made DC seem like a very manufactured place.

A LITTLE LIFE
DISRUPTING CLASS
Henry Kissinger
On China

When and why did you decide to become an architect?

My mother's father, who was an orthodontist, liked to build furniture in his spare time. I spent a lot of time in his house admiring his work. Hearing stories about how he built his own bathroom, with the help of his children, I was always fascinated by construction and design. I was going to be a doctor, like my parents, but at Harvard I decided to switch majors from biology to visual and environmental studies, a change that enabled me to take a lot of architecture courses. I took a studio course with Albert Szabo (one of the faculty advisors to Le Corbusier on the design of the Carpenter Center), who later advised my thesis. I learned many things from him, particularly important principles about inhabitation, light, and the shifting of scale as it relates to circulation. He always advised against designing spaces that were too constricted: "Never create a space where cats can crawl in and die."

In the summer before my senior year in college I studied the history of Renaissance art and architecture in Florence. There I met a group of architecture students who were from Northeastern University along with their instructor. I ended up joining them, and we traveled around Europe to many great cities and buildings, including Ronchamp, the Villa Savoye, and the works of Gaudi in Barcelona. That got me more excited to continue my study of architecture. I also worked for a year for Kallmann McKinnell and Wood, making models and drawing details and generally becoming immersed in the life of an architecture office, which furthered my interest. So I decided to apply to architecture school.

And when you got to the Harvard Graduate School of Design, what were some of your most important influences there?

I did a research thesis, in which I looked at the work of Steven Holl and Enric Miralles. The latter taught at GSD and was hugely influential then. My advisor, George Baird, had written a book called *The Space of Appearance*, which addressed the philosophy of phenomenology not just in terms of the sensorial and haptic, like qualities of light, but the actual physical effects of space. Research for my thesis touched on Hannah Arendt's work—how different types of social interactions create space, and how design can foster social interactions. I analyzed Holl's Fukuoka apartments and the Igualada Cemetery by Miralles, looking at different scales of circulation—the public-scale circulation versus the smaller human-scale circulation—and how they intersect each other and serve as traces of inhabitation. So I looked at those two projects in terms of how they were defining different kinds of occupation, public versus individual.

One key text for me was Robin Evans's 1978 essay "Figures, Doors and Passages," which traces the history of circulation, addressing the history of circulation in building design and analyzing artwork to examine the way that sightlines from figures in the works produce space. Beatriz Colomina's text, "The Split Wall: Domestic Voyeurism" about the Adolf Loos houses, was just published [in 1997] at the time I was working on my thesis and was also influential. It analyzes the connections between visual sightlines and physical circulation paths—the paths you move along versus the axes your eyes follow. This text led me to Walter Benjamin's 1939 text "Paris, Capital of the Nineteenth Century," where he initiates the entire discussion about inhabitation and the traces of different kinds of inhabitants on architectural space.

color photography
ANIMALS
HIRSCHFELD
DINOSAURS

ORIENTATIONS

With a nod to theorist Catherine Ingraham's work on architecture and the animal as well as geographer Nigel Thrift's work on the post-human, you've spoken about your work as being an "other"-oriented architecture. What do you mean by that?

I'd say I'm interested in different kinds of occupants—not only grown-up people but also children as well as animals. Machines could be in that category too; think about the emerging typology of the data center. In the past, the most important way that the built environment supported the broader culture was the way in which architecture was scaled to fit certain inhabitants. But the assumption that the most important subject is always an adult human is quickly shifting. For example, there's this whole advertising campaign in the New York City subways right now encouraging New Yorkers to recognize other New Yorkers, which in this case are pictured as deer and raccoons. That reflects a very different mindset from the old we-live-here, those-are-pests approach: you can acknowledge the presence of the natural world or the non-living (machine) world, and accommodate it.

How did you find yourself first becoming interested in this approach?

I have been teaching at Pratt since 2001, when the Masters in Architecture program was first introduced. In 2009, I taught a studio where we were exploring interventions into East River Park. One student in particular became interested in pigeons, and his project turned into this giant housing scheme for birds. That was really interesting. That was definitely the first instance where I was advising a student on a project for something other than a human inhabitant.

In my mind I started thinking: what does it mean to shift the subject of architecture, especially in terms of shifting the tools and the methods of architectural fabrication? Look at the first page of any graphic standards manual, and you can see evidence of people inhabiting different levels of scale; or look at the size of a residential hallway, which is always a little wider than your body. But then look closer at what actually ends up inhabiting so many of those spaces: not only the projected inhabitants, but also objects, machines, equipment, animals, and plants. So as both an academic and a practitioner, I kept thinking about that pigeon project, speculating about other possible inhabitants for spaces and the techniques that could be applied to produce them.

So, at the outset you were thinking of this shift as being applicable on a very large scale?

Absolutely. The potential for this approach is all the more important given that we're trying to bring vegetation back into urban environments and accommodate urban wildlife, while we are densifying the occupation of these spaces. We need to be able to program infrastructure in more than one way. If a project's priority, for example, is vehicular transportation, then how do we utilize the adjacent areas surrounding it? Infrastructural projects from the Robert Moses era in New York were engineered for a single type of use, whereas earlier projects, like the Brooklyn Bridge, actually accommodated more than one type of use (pedestrian, bicycle, and vehicular). A recent, more inventive approach would be something like the Low Line Park, which activates the space around and under a roadbed for activities and uses apart from transportation.

We've tried applying this idea at similar scale ourselves in our speculative proposal for a project called "Chromatic Energy Landscape," the brief for which was to design a work of land art cum energy generator. It intrigued me because the project, very big

in scale, provided an opportunity to look towards the making of an infrastructural space that was a navigable environment as well as a cultural destination. The site was in the desert in Dubai, adjacent to a wildlife sanctuary. Our primary energy-generating strategy was based on a project in the Mojave Desert, which consisted of light-sensitive reflectors that focus solar energy onto conduit tubes that then feed centralized generators. We also designed a secondary layer of algae ponds that could be harvested for biofuel, basing the layout on a drawing by MC Escher. There were two overlapping "layers" to our thinking as well: the first was the use of color, which was a way to bring the project into the realm of art, and the second was how to relate the complex to the wildlife sanctuary. On the color front, we came up with design elements, whereby the reflectors, coated in dichroic paint so that they appear to change color as you're walking by, could be angled into different positions, adding some visual variation. Their varying angles allowed them to double as "bird hides"—like the opposite of a duck blind, a place to conceal humans so that they could observe the birdlife. Even though the idea of connecting the project to the wildlife sanctuary wasn't in the brief, it added something to the landscape by helping it accommodate not only different kinds of human users but also a whole different population, the birds themselves.

So then at the smaller scale, in your built work, how has this kind of "otherness" been addressed?

In the townhouse for a poet-artist couple and their cats, we designed an entire fifty-foot-wall for their books and other belongings. In the process we realized that it could also be configured to accommodate the cats, affording them alternative ways to travel from level to level. The cats are playful, but don't like strangers, so the wall of books on display incorporates steps that allow the cats to go up and down via a continuous undulating ledge, which leads to two trap doors, so they can move between floors. There's a layering of ideas surrounding display, storage and another kind of circulation.

The Maple Street School is another example—this time addressing spaces for children rather than animals. A set of openings scaled for adults is placed above another set for children, creating a horizontally layered datum for each group. We designed the school's kitchen to be a social gathering space that looks like a food truck, with a service counter opposite the preparation area. This counter (which doubles as a stage) is scaled down to child-seating height. In a preschool the bathroom is part of the learning experience, a place where you're teaching the children about hygiene. The adults need to be able to supervise, but the children also need privacy, so there are apertures in the bathroom enclosure that allow different viewing angles. The sink area incorporates various programmatic uses: it's for cleaning up but also flows out into the main space and becomes a place for play. That puts a special emphasis on that part of the training—washing your hands can be something kids are usually reluctant to do—by connecting it to the idea of play. No chore is fun, but you can make learning and playing two sides of the same thing, by inventing a system that connects them.

THE ASSEMBLY

The "assembly" is another idea you return to a lot. It appears to be a sort of armature that you insert into a space, and that insertion simultaneously facilitates different functions at different scales. Could you expand on that?

I consider that term as being distinct from the artistic idea of *assemblage*: an assembly is not something freestanding, but a bundling together of elements to capitalize on space, while also maintaining openness, expansiveness, and densification. It's an attempt to connect one context, scale and use to another—display with seating, for instance—creating a hybridization of the program. In the school, the kitchen and bathroom volumes operate as types of assemblies that combine scale and use. In other types of projects, like the office and the retail projects, there is often more of a spatial segregation. You can also see the assembly at work in our project for the poet-and-cats house: the shelves are basically projecting out, becoming almost a stair, something somewhere between furniture and part of the building—a blurring of categories between the two.

How have you deployed assemblies elsewhere?

In the brownstone project we did for multiple generations of one family the assembly concept bundles different uses together, particularly around circulation spaces, which are abundant in this house, leading us to nickname it "the house of seven stairs." It's designed for three generations to live within one building, each with its own spaces. There's a pied-à-terre for the owner and his wife, which shares a kitchen with the top unit on floors three and four. The stairs we added, to pair the floors together and create duplexes, became assembly devices. Each of these stairs is materially distinct and activates its surroundings differently. The parlor floor has a linear stair that runs along the party wall to connect it to the second floor. A storage space, a sort of niche-office nook, and a kitchen are all carved into the space below the stair. Between the third and fourth floors, the stair is actually located against the front facade. It is made of painted

perforated metal, and light comes through, turning it into a sculptural focal point and a sort of brise-soleil, with a window seat and bookshelf tucked underneath it. Lined with wood like a piece of cabinetry, the one that goes between the garden level and the cellars incorporates a bench seat on one level and an open shelf storage below it. The sky-lit stairs lead to the roof deck with shelves adjacent to the landing, where plants can get light.

We often alternate between inserting things into spaces and carving spaces out—or even deleting spaces to "wedge" more functionality into a project. The son, who lives in the top duplex, wanted to display all of his belongings, so we designed his space like a retail environment. Because he is developing a new food product, the kitchen is a huge, open-shelf layout, almost like a laboratory. To make enough space for cooking and eating, we restricted the living room to a seating alcove under the stairs. The daughter, living on the parlor floor duplex, is a restaurateur who is also always testing out recipes. We found a way to fit her kitchen and dining area onto the same side as the garden, to give it easy outdoor access for al fresco dining and cooking. In a way, the cellar level actually turned out to be the most fun because we carved away the rear facade to expose the arched brick support wall. The arched openings lead to different support spaces, like an office/study, bathroom, and a closet.

So the assembly is an instrument of economy, of maximizing functional potential?

It's not necessarily about squeezing use into every available space. In the brownstone's case, the assembly creates spatial sequences that organize and interweave different uses and scales, as well as bridge furniture and architecture, circulation and rooms, moving and viewing. Stairs are both a functional conveyance from floor to floor and a registration of the scale of the inhabitant. The scale of the steps is the most specific to human dimensions and helps one understand the scale of a space or a drawing. Playing with the spatial sequence of movement and the (often contrasting) spatial sequence of visual connections or sightlines is an old game in architecture. Coming from landscape architecture—the promenade—it plays out in urban projects, as well as in waterfront projects, where sightline trajectories connect the inside with the outside, while circulation sequences bring interior spaces together. That the assembly can make all these processes and forms of habitation visible—that's an idea very much informed, for me, by some of those theoretical sources from my academic background, thinkers like Robin Evans and Walter Benjamin, the latter of which notably wrote, "To live is to leave traces."

PRACTICE AND PEDAGOGY

You maintain one foot firmly planted in the academy, and the other in the "real" world of building actual buildings. What's the impulse behind this sort of professional dualism?

When I was at the Harvard Graduate School of Design (GSD), Toshiko Mori was hired as the Robert P. Hubbard Professor in Practice. She became a model for me, particularly after I began working for her before going out on my own. The faculty also included big names like Herzog & de Meuron and Enric Miralles, European practitioners who had returned to academia after professional success. I started to wonder: where will my practice lie in the spectrum between practice and academia? I was interested in coming back to teach, but I soon realized that I was committed to seeing how ideas could be translated into built work.

After graduating, I specifically sought out small practices that were well connected academically. While working for Toshiko, I started teaching at Pratt, three years after I graduated, and she was hugely supportive. It was an easy way for me to test out how to straddle both worlds. I came to realize that experience in practice could exert influence on teaching, and bringing concepts and abstract thinking, borrowed from academia, into concrete form could pave the way for new ideas to enter practice.

It could be said that, coming from the GSD, you already had a certain pragmatic outlook—since the program has, traditionally at least, a hands-on quality. How has that affected your thinking, and how has it changed in the years since?

It wasn't until I started teaching at Pratt that I became aware how much the GSD had shaped my outlook on architecture. Harvard had been so European in its outlook, and was slower to adopt digital design strategies. I had become particularly interested in the digital realm—but the GSD had only gotten a 3D printer at the very end of my time there. At Pratt, I suddenly found myself mixed in with a group of young professors who graduated from Columbia's Graduate School

of Architecture, Planning, and Preservation (GSAPP) and had been through paperless studios that focused on exploring digital media, led then by Dean Bernard Tschumi. By teaching alongside them I was exposed to their experience and influences. The inaugural Pratt Graduate Architecture and Urban Design Chair, Catherine Ingraham, and the second chair, Bill MacDonald, took the digital agenda that had begun at Columbia and continued to advance it at Pratt. The post-digital agenda is still evolving, as the school continues to embrace new ideas. Over the 16-plus years I have been engaged in academia, I have come to realize that teaching allows you to keep educating yourself and contributing ideas to the discourse.

So how do some of the abstract notions you explore in the classroom inform your day-to-day work in the studio—and/or how does your studio work play back into your conceptual thinking?

One thing you definitely learn in practice is how to deal with constraints, which often times become the meat of the whole project. In an urban environment, the context can be highly specific and potentially restrictive. I've learned to look for the opportunities in constraints and even seek them out—as with the bird sanctuary, where we settled on the constraint of this "other-ized" subject. In some cases, the constraint could be imagining the client as a bird, but it could be that the clients have unusual requests—cat-loving poets being a perfect example. Some think the best kind of project is for a big developer, without strong personalities and subjective inputs. But often, in great projects, the personalities *make* the project.

I find that what you learn in the academy never goes away. Thinking about the idea of context: at the GSD, William J. R. Curtis's text on the Spanish architects Enric Miralles and Carme Pinós was a key reference for my thesis. He describes their projects as "mental maps and social landscapes," where circulation threads through a complex context so that the circulation itself becomes the generator of social space, a notion that really circles back to the assembly idea that I am thinking about today. Having a space in the classroom to explore big ideas helps me as a designer. In the world of academia, you can choose the scale you want work in, and that makes tackling larger projects in the studio less daunting—like, for example, the speculative project we did called the Tirana Exchange Center, an intermodal transport hub with circulation sequences that weave through space and layers of different programs, including a walking rail and a bike path. We're also working on a multi-unit residential development facing Prospect Park, which will be the first time that we'll have tackled that typology in a commissioned project. All this is familiar terrain by now, since I've been working out these ideas for so long in the classroom—one more reason I don't have much anxiety about scaling up.

20TH STREET HOUSE

This 20-foot-wide wood frame townhouse, located at the end of a row along a narrow side yard, had existing front and rear extensions. The building volume was selectively manipulated—in some cases through addition, in others through subtraction—to improve room sizes, sequences, and adjacencies. Generously sized skylights, window walls, and glazed corners were employed to make the most of available natural light.

The front extension was carved away at the corner to create a covered front porch, wraparound window, and mudroom. The rotation of the front door—now perpendicular to the street—attenuates the entry sequence (meaning the visitor doesn't enter directly into the main volume, as in a typical row house). To open up the exposed wall to available light, the stairs were relocated to the party wall. Instead of a straight run, the stairs take a 90-degree turn and are lit from above by a large skylight. The corners of the living room and dining rooms were eroded to bring light in and extend views diagonally.

The rear extension was widened to about 15 feet to create a generous mahogany-paneled kitchen with an island, pantry and home office nook. A deck off the kitchen extends the materiality of the interior living spaces out into the yard. Upstairs, the master suite is located at the front and insulated from the bustle of the house by an airlock of two parallel pocket doors. A windowed walk-in closet, sky-lit bathroom, and west-facing glazed wall allow lots of light inside. In the back, corner-wrapping windows take advantage of the open skies behind the house to bring generous amounts of light into the children's bedrooms. White oak, used for floors, stairs, and built-in shelving and cabinets throughout the house keep the palette pale and neutral.

In the bathrooms, oak elements mix with cement tile and ceramic mosaics in blue and white. In the basement, which is set up as a family room and equipment storage space, vinyl tiles in a graphic pattern provide visual interest. Outside, tongue and groove white cedar siding, paired with integrated fencing and planters, creates crisp square corners. Rectangles of gray stain wrap the corners and insets to emphasize the volumetric shifts in the facade.

638

REEVE PLACE HOUSE

Reeve Place House is 25 feet wide and also at the end of a row, with a side driveway. A two-story hayloft, re-clad in stucco, occupies a corner of the rear yard. The house was razed to its foundations—including a garage demolished to increase the size of the fenced rear yard—and then rebuilt as a light-filled, cedar-clad structure with diagonal views of Prospect Park a short distance away. An entry porch was carved from the southeast corner and the front turns to face the driveway rather than the street. A secondary porch at the northwest corner allows access to the house from the rear yard via a mudroom off of the kitchen. The northeast corner of the house is sliced at an angle, allowing light to penetrate into the yard.

Inside, the open-plan living-dining-kitchen space includes a mix of minimal modern detailing and richly textured reclaimed elements. The loft-like volume of the living space incorporates reclaimed wooden ceiling beams, original walnut floors, and a bluestone-wrapped gas fireplace. The grand walnut-clad stair that spills into the space has a stainless steel balustrade. A basement floor was converted to a rec room with a floating projection wall separating social space from storage.

The second floor is divided into children's and parent's wings separated by a pocket door and laundry station. In front, the master suite has a bedroom with wraparound views toward the park, though a mature locust tree provides some privacy. A large sky-lit bath with a windowed shower room and walk-in closet, also windowed, complete the suite. The children's rooms are distinguished by the chamfered roofline at the rear of the house.

PROSPECT PARK DEVELOPMENT, BROOKLYN

The owners of a small house on a fantastic lot overlooking Prospect Park needed to expand to house their extended family. Lot restrictions had kept them from making the necessary expansions, but then the lot directly behind them became available for sale. A discussion with another neighbor led to another offer to sell. The owners approached us to partner up on the design and financing of a proposal to develop the resulting 3,700-square-foot lot with a FAR of 3 into a nine-unit, 11,100-square-foot, five-story building.

The front facade is comprised of cast aluminum and CFRG panels, the product of a collaboration with Brooklyn-based Situ Fabrication. The concept for the front facade is to create a unique window out of a kit of parts of window shapes and panels for each room facing the park as well as the penthouse skylights. Windows tilt at slight angles to direct different views of the Park. The top three levels also enjoy vistas out toward the bay and the Statue of Liberty.

Inside, one-, two-, and three-bedroom units occupy four elevator-accessible floors, with the penthouse level reserved for the family and grandparents. The unit partitions can be modified to give bedrooms to one unit or the other on the same floor. On the first floor, duplexes make use of below-grade space. White oak surfaces the floors and accent walls of the living spaces.

3-LOT COMBINATION
45 + 46 + 46A PROSPECT PARK SOUTHWEST

3,188 SF LOT AREA

3.0 FAR

9,563 SF MAX. FLOOR AREA

60 - 70 FT. HIGH

5 STORY PLUS ROOF DECK

NINE UNITS:

ONE 4-BEDROOM UNIT

ONE 3-BEDROOM UNIT

THREE 2-BEDROOM UNITS

THREE 2-BEDROOM UNITS

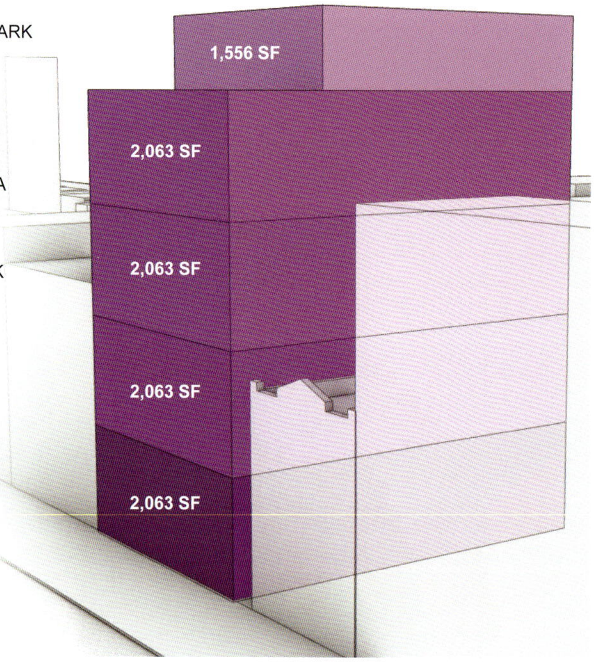

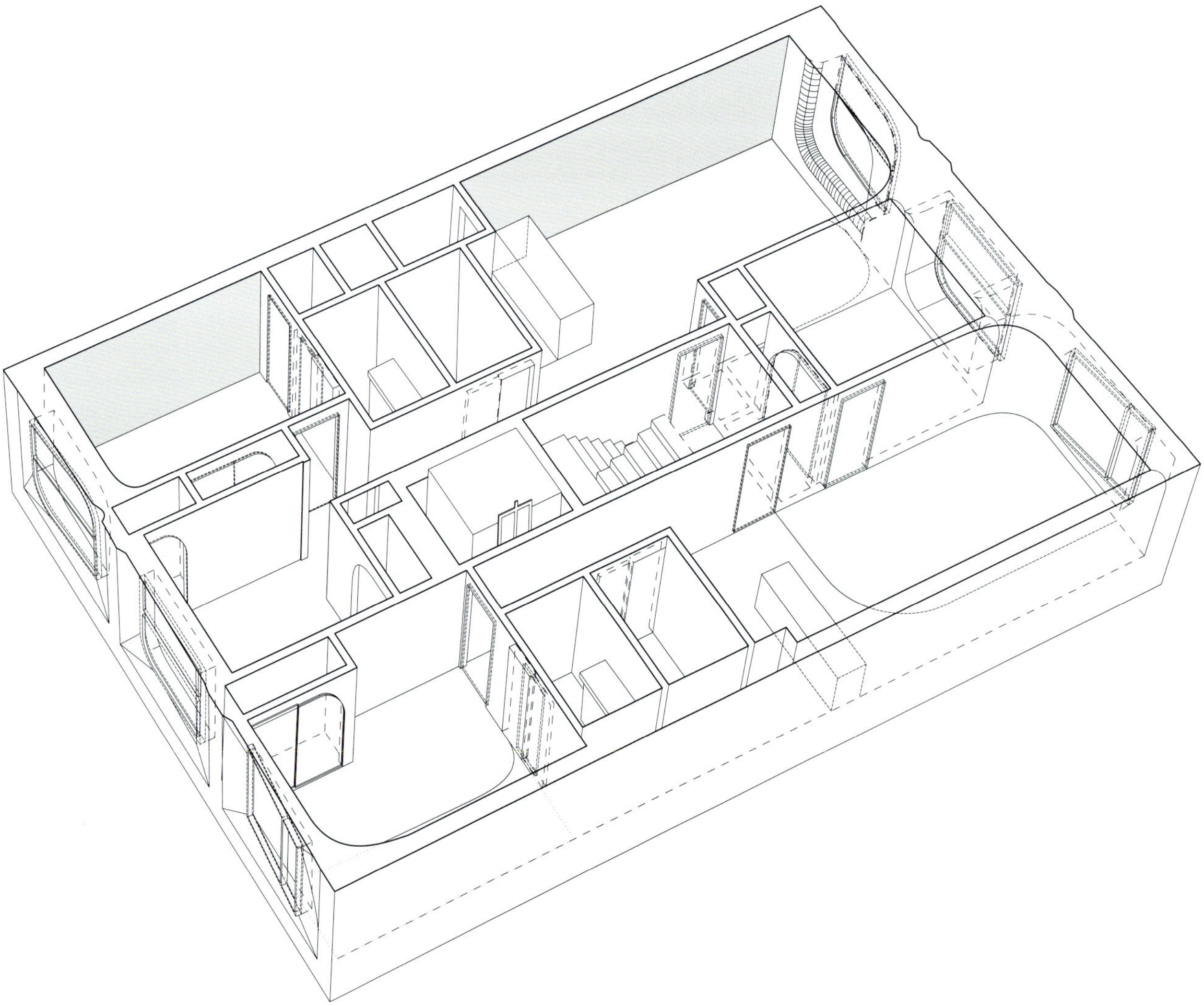

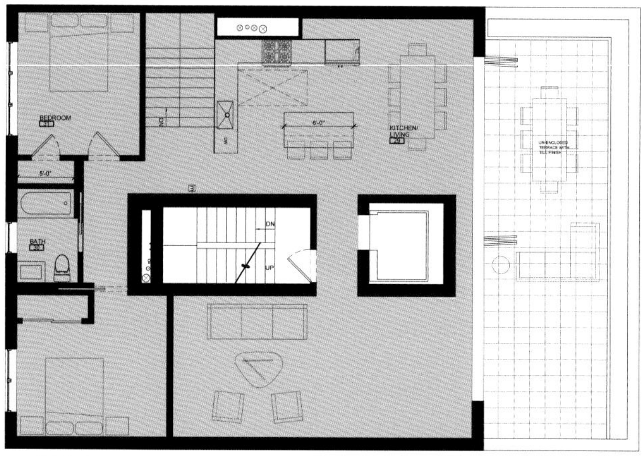

PENTHOUSE FLOOR PLAN

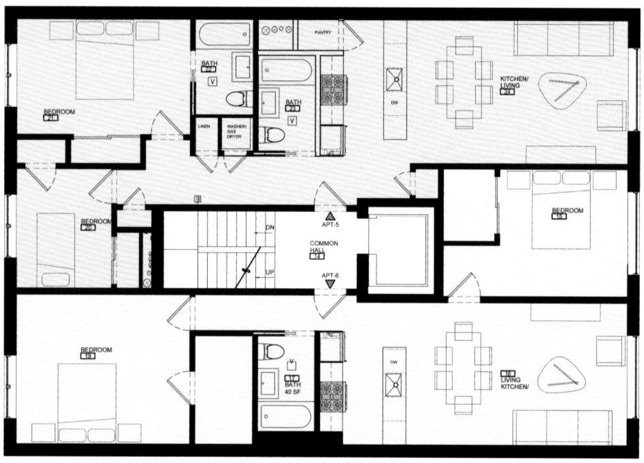

THIRD FLOOR PLAN

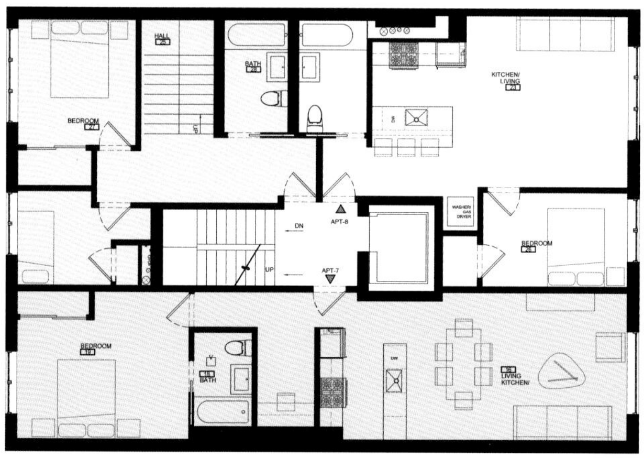

FOURTH FLOOR PLAN

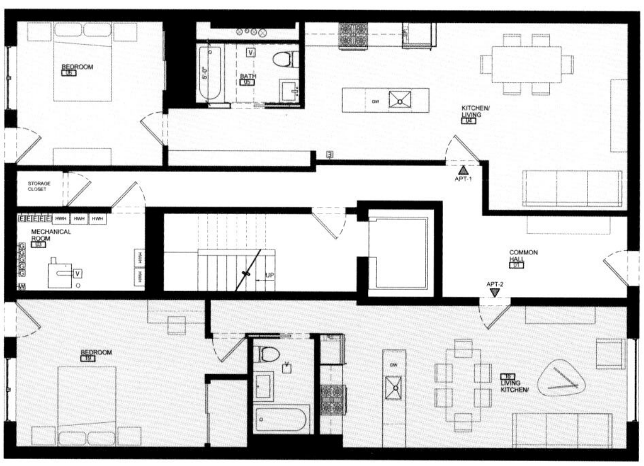

FIRST FLOOR PLAN

SECOND FLOOR PLAN

FORT GREENE BROWNSTONE

A Hong Kong-based businessman, the father of three adult children, purchased this brownstone in a Brooklyn landmark district. His goal was to create a pied-à-terre for himself and his wife, and homes for the three children, all under one roof.

Extended meetings with each family member resulted in a plan for three duplex apartments for the children and an efficiency unit for the parents. That required the creation of three new stairways, one within each duplex. The new stairs became not just sculptural elements inside the units but programmatic focal points, gathering shelving, built-in seating, and office alcoves in and around them.

The eldest daughter, a restaurateur, lives on the parlor and second floors with her husband and their child. The house's original ten-foot-tall mahogany doors open into their living room. The large kitchen and dining room overlook a rear deck through a wall of windows. An interior window in the dining room brings light into the common hallway and allows a glimpse from that hallway through the living spaces and into the rear yard. Inside the unit, an oak-clad, straight-run stair leading to the second floor forms a thick wall containing storage space and a desk in an oak-lined recess. At the top of the stairs are a master suite in front and a child's suite in back.

The youngest child, a food entrepreneur, and his partner, an artist, occupy the third and fourth floors. His goal for the unit was to create an environment where everything was on display.

The open shelves of the upper and lower kitchen cabinets showcase the couple's extensive collection of cooking supplies and appliances, used for experiments in creating nutritious packaged foods. In an unusual move, the stair to the second floor was located at the front of the room, allowing the dining table to occupy the center of the space. Painted, perforated steel forms a diaphanous railing that allows light from the front windows to pass through into the space. Tucked under the stair is a window seat with storage and shelving—the unit's only nod to a proper living room.

Upstairs, a recessed aluminum track and bracket system fitted with custom white oak shelves lines the walls, putting clothing and personal items on display. Racks of gym equipment share space with a library wall. The custom white oak platform bed and headboard are stacked with more volumes.

The third sibling has a basement duplex surfaced in wide-plank white oak. On the upper level, a bench flanks the opening to the stair, which winds down to land in a wood-lined walk-in closet. The arched brick supports of the building's central foundation wall frame open into a study and a bathroom enclosed by a pair of custom mahogany doors.

181

The parents' suite includes a bedroom and bathroom with custom wallpaper based on art by the son's partner. A pocket door allows direct access to the son's kitchen.

A deep blue color is used as an organizing thread within the units as well as in the common spaces, which include a roof deck and shared cellar. The blue entry doors open into a foyer with a blue handrail that snakes up to the blue-fenced roof terrace. The blue reappears in the railing and stairs accessing the rear yard and deck.

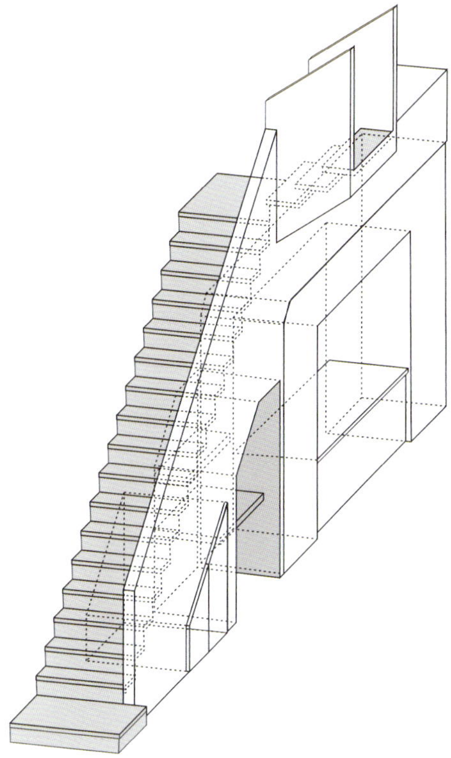

RESTAURANT
DIM SUM
SUGAR AND SWEETS
ROASTING
infuse
ROBERT KURSON
SHADOW DIVERS
ZADIE SMITH
WILLIAM GIBSON
CURRY
THE FLAVOR BIBLE

WOLF

MINA STONE COOKING FOR ARTISTS

CHUCK CLOSE

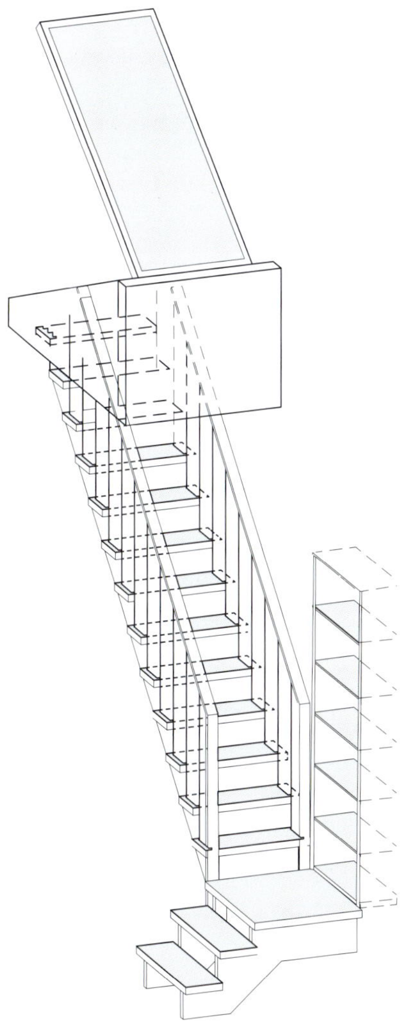

德雁坊

12-FOOT-WIDE HOUSE

This 12-foot-wide Brooklyn row house arrays a family's life on four narrow but light-filled levels. A new switchback stair sets up a dialogue between the front spaces, which preserve as many nineteenth-century details as possible, and those in the rear, where a two-story addition culminates in oversized "storefront system" windows. The clients, married professionals with two small children, wanted an open, flowing living space. While they wouldn't—and couldn't—alter the original brick street front, with its vaguely gothic details, they wanted the house to be as bright as possible.

The living spaces occupy the parlor floor. The distinctive window in the southwest-facing brick facade brings light into the living room. Although the entry vestibule, with its existing flooring, was preserved, the wall between the vestibule and the living room, which constricted both spaces, was removed so that the new steel and oak stair divides the living room from the L-shaped kitchen and the dining area, which occupy the extension.

Apertures visually expand the narrow space. The rear glass facade allows a view from the entry straight through to the backyard. Meanwhile, an opening in the wall of the stairwell creates a diagonal sightline from the entry up through the second-floor study and out a window door leading to the second-floor roof deck. The stairway, flanked by vertical wooden slats on one side and exposed brick on the other, feels integral to both the original building and the addition.

The master suite occupies the front of the second floor. An existing fireplace mantel is preserved as a reminder of the building's history. Closets line the hallway opposite the stair, with the bathroom and study opening onto the roof deck at the back. The third (and top) floor contains the children's bedrooms, at front and back, with a shared, sky-lit bathroom between them.

On the garden (ground) level, the stair separates the family room in front from an au pair's suite in back. Outside, a spiral stair leads to a deck off of the dining room. A wooden fence wraps the perimeter of the yard, merging into the cedar siding of the extension, connecting the house to its surroundings.

365A

HOUSE FOR BOOKLOVERS AND CATS

The clients, one an artist, poet, and professor, and her husband, an administrator at the Library of Congress, asked us to convert this Brooklyn row house into a series of lively, light-filled spaces. They also wanted the house to accommodate their two shy but inquisitive cats—with ways for the cats to slip away from unexpected guests.

The key feature of the reconfigured house is an airy, parlor-floor living space. The 20-by-50-foot room is bordered by bookshelves configured around cat circulation routes. Shelves project to create steps for the cats to climb up to a continuous open ledge where they can observe activities below. Trap doors allow the cats to access second-floor rooms at either end of the house. Inset in the shelf wall is a diorama designed by the owner of a living room concealed behind a front door painted to match the front door of the house. Other recesses, some painted in Benjamin Moore's Melon Popsicle, house the owners' collections of small objects. A central skylight brings light through the second floor to the main living space.

The floor is organized into four separate areas—the living room, media room, dining area, and kitchen—that pinwheel around the functional wall floating in the middle of the space, which defines a hallway zone that provides access to the powder room and basement. On the other side, the wall defines the media room seating area, and also screens the kitchen in the back from the living room in the front.

At the back of the house, a two-story wall of glass floods the interior with light. Outside, stairs lead down to the rear yard.

On the second floor, a studio for the artist/poet occupies the back half of the house. A balcony projecting from the window wall allows the client to step outside for quick breaks from work. In the corner is her sky-lit "nest"—a partially concealed, elevated space to write and think in. The structure is formed from dimensional lumber and wood elements recycled from the house.

Below grade is a "cat free zone" intended for guests. The front room is configured as a workout space. A guest suite occupies the back; a glass door provides access to the newly landscaped rear yard. Splashes of color in the form of yellow-hued columns and a green bench keep the lower level bright and inviting.

Materials in the original house were recycled whenever possible. The existing paneled wood doors, doorknobs, and hardware were reused and the pine flooring was refinished. An antique wood storage unit was incorporated into the new shelving wall. Paints and finishes emphasize original details wherever possible.

NINA KATCHADOURIAN CURIOUSER

SURFBOARD HOUSE

Five years after Hurricane Sandy wreaked havoc on the coastline of New York City, the Surfboard House was completed. The owners of the house on Reeve Place in Brooklyn hired us to build a beach house a short drive away. They had purchased a lot in Breezy Point, a beachfront community with a cooperative structure in Queens. The waterfront lot was the site of a house that had been washed away by the Hurricane. Houses in Breezy Point are set close together and linked by pedestrian paths; cars are confined to lots at the periphery. The clients' site was unusually wide, with 68 feet of south-facing beach frontage. Flood regulations required building at least six feet off of the ground, while co-op regulations put the maximum building height at 28 feet. The co-op also required a setback from the lot line of 32 feet at the lot's widest point. The resulting building envelope was much shallower than wide, allowing nearly every room to have an ocean view. One of the primary design strategies was stepping the south-facing facade to allow windows to wrap corners. That created diagonal sightlines up and down the beach, framing vistas, and visually expanding the interior spaces. Angled roof profiles and ceiling finishes also direct the eye upward and outward.

Access to the house is provided in two places. A stair leading from the beach lands on a deck that spans the width of the house. The west side of the house abuts a pedestrian pathway. A separate switchback stair provides access to the side entrance, which slides between volumes corresponding to the living room and an indoor–outdoor bath/shower. Because it is accessible from outside, that sky-lit bathroom provides a place to rinse off and deposit bathing suits and towels before entering the house.

These two entrances flank the living room volume, which is defined by a raised cedar-clad ceiling; nine-foot tall, south-facing sliding glass doors; and a diagonally pitched roof. Across from the dining area, the kitchen abuts the stair to the second floor in an L-shaped alcove. The clients wanted separate zones for adult and children to live and entertain in. That was accomplished by locating the master suite on the main floor so that the children could have the second floor to themselves.

On the east side, the master bedroom has wraparound windows toward undeveloped beach frontage. A bathroom and walk-in closet buffer the bedroom from a parking lot to the north. A level change allows part of the deck to connect directly to the master suite.

Upstairs, three small bedrooms feel expansive thanks to their corner views. A rec room opens onto a covered deck. The fiberglass-wrapped roof culminates in a large "surfboard-like" overhang that protects the first floor from solar heat gain. White cedar cladding wraps the building and roof overhangs and encases the sides of the deck.

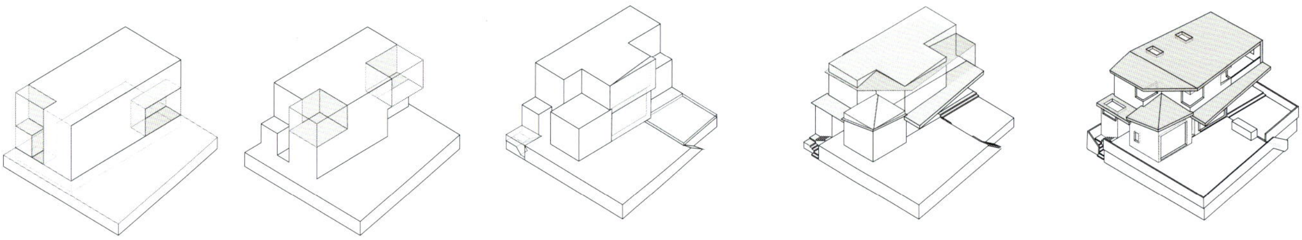

DEEP POINT HOUSE

A 1950s ranch house failed to make the most of its 17-acre site overlooking two converging creeks. The owners wanted to enlarge the house and take advantage of the sweeping vistas and light reflected off the water. The house was torn down to its foundation, which had to be kept in part due to the building's proximity to the water. The Chesapeake Bay Act would have required that a new structure shift significantly away from the shore.

A new entry on the east facade divides the original south-facing volume from the den extension to the north, creating a breezeway with a water view and access to a wraparound desk. An exterior stair continues the breezeway sequence, which culminates in a rooftop garden. Inside, the living spaces feature a three-sided, storefront-like glass enclosure offering views to the south, west, and north, with large sliding doors leading to the deck. The open plan of the kitchen, living, and dining rooms is punctuated by a two-sided fireplace, which separates dining and living areas. Skylights on either side allow light to bounce off the surface of the chimney volume. The L-shaped kitchen has a 12-foot-long island, topped in Namibian white marble—the same material used for both fireplace surrounds.

Adjacent guest bedrooms are located at the eastern end of the first floor; each offers sweeping waterfront vistas. The bathroom for one of them doubles as a powder room for guests.

The den wing has been extended to incorporate an interior stair leading to the new second floor master suite. In the master bathroom, the tub is raised up two steps in the northwest corner of the bathroom to afford bathers a multidirectional treetop view. A skylight over the bed washes the yellow wall behind the headboard in light. Outside, planted rows of herbs and flowers comprise a "capsule farm" on the rooftop. The flora delineates an outdoor seating area while giving the master bedroom added privacy.

MAPLE STREET SCHOOL

Maple Street School, designed collaboratively with 4Mativ Design Studio, occupies the second floor of a new mixed-use development in Brooklyn. The program called for three interconnected classrooms with an emphasis on social gathering spaces. Large sliding partitions, a shared multipurpose room, and roof play space allow for a variety of interactions among groups of children. The choice of maple for floors, walls, and ceilings, as well as for built-in and freestanding furniture, gives the space warmth and visual unity, and alludes to the school's name. Touches of color frame the openings between rooms in unexpected and playful ways. At the entry, a maple pegboard with colorful pegs entertains children, while their parents are occupied at the front desk.

The school's practice of scheduling "cafe times," daily group gatherings centered on snacks, led the designers to organize the multipurpose space and cubby area around a central kitchen. Modeled after a food truck, it has a service window and counter for adults to use, as well as a counter at toddler-height that folds in when not in use. An acrylic panel displays the daily menu.

Pairs of tall maple pocket doors, with oval cutouts at different heights to give children and adults views between spaces, partition the classrooms. When the pocket doors are opened, the rooms become a single space for school-wide events. Bathrooms aren't hidden away but rather inserted into the classrooms spaces. Views are controlled so that teachers can supervise but children feel a sense of privacy. On the outside walls of the bathrooms, interconnecting play sinks give the children a peek into the adjacent classrooms. Touches of color appear in the porcelain tile that lines the bathrooms and the play sinks.

On the roof, rubber tiles patterned to suggest islands in water are framed by a combination of warm cedar fencing and a patchwork of perforated aluminum screens.

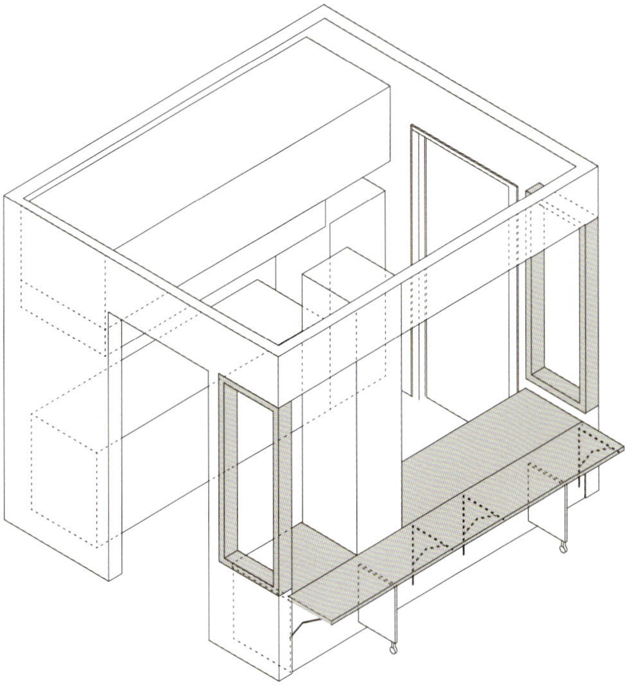

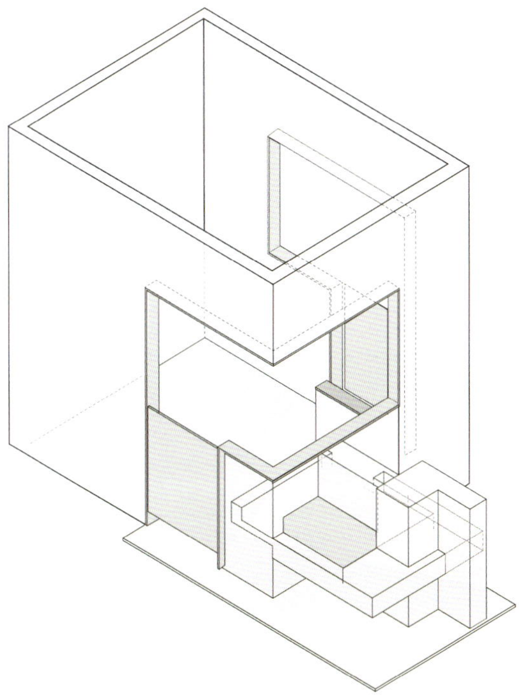

MAPS
DRAGONS
LEGO

BOLLARE OFFICE

Bollare, a Los Angeles-based public relations firm, was expanding its presence in Manhattan. The firm approached us with a site in a landmarked Tribeca warehouse that had never been converted to offices, and a mood board that featured an eclectic mix of materials, patterns, and furniture channeling California beach culture. Bollare required an open area that could contain desks but also work as a showroom for fashion clients and enclosed spaces housing a photography studio, VIP lounge, executive offices, and meeting rooms.

The strategy for the open space was to keep the palette and finishes neutral in order to showcase the heavy timber framing, wood surfaces, and brick walls of the existing structure. The maple floors were treated with a clear finish, while the ceiling joists and columns were sanded and painted. Electrical outlets, placed strategically in the floor, provide flexibility for desks and clothing racks. Strip lighting and spots on different circuits allow for ambient (office) or directed (showroom) illumination.

In contrast, the enclosed spaces received a much higher level of finish, while maintaining flexible configurations and visual connections. The executive offices are set behind a wall of glass that allows natural light from the building's windows to pass into the showroom. Garage door openings in the studio and VIP lounge "facades" allow activities to spill out into the showroom. Playful details double as photo opportunities, including a green wall and a neon company sign. "Aloha" is spelled out in tile as a kind of mosaic welcome mat and background for shoe selfies, or "shoefies."

EXIT

BODY FACTORY

This project takes the idea of a "mullet strategy," where a design conforms to normative forms and proportions at its public face and reverts to a more dynamic spatial logic on its private face and reverses it to draw in visitors. A dramatically lit, eye-catching retail space for Dermalogica, an award-winning skincare line, leads to a series of private therapy rooms in back. The retail space is a tall, faceted enclosure of triangular panels surfaced in troweled concrete, visible to passers-by through storefront windows. In the gaps between them, LED tape lights illuminate the panels indirectly. Floors are polished concrete. Along the sidewalls, products line the floating acrylic shelving units; the shelves themselves are edge-lit by hidden LEDs. Overhead, a custom triangular LED light fixture frames the edge of the paneled surface where it stops to expose the ceiling. The reception desk was custom designed and fabricated out of white Caesarstone in a faceted pattern to complement the walls.

The paneled surface splits to create an entrance to a cove-lit corridor with treatment rooms on either side. Direct lighting in the rooms comes from large round lenses set in the lowered ceiling, while indirect lighting emerges from perimeter coves, which also conceal air supply vents. The walls—where not concealed by full-height counter and storage units—are covered in wallpaper with a linear, textured pattern.

The bathroom at the end of the hall is covered completely in black penny tile with a backlit mirror providing illumination. One treatment room features a shower lined in white and gray penny tiles. Access to a mezzanine through an office provides additional storage and space for technicians.

SKIN CARE

SKIN CARE

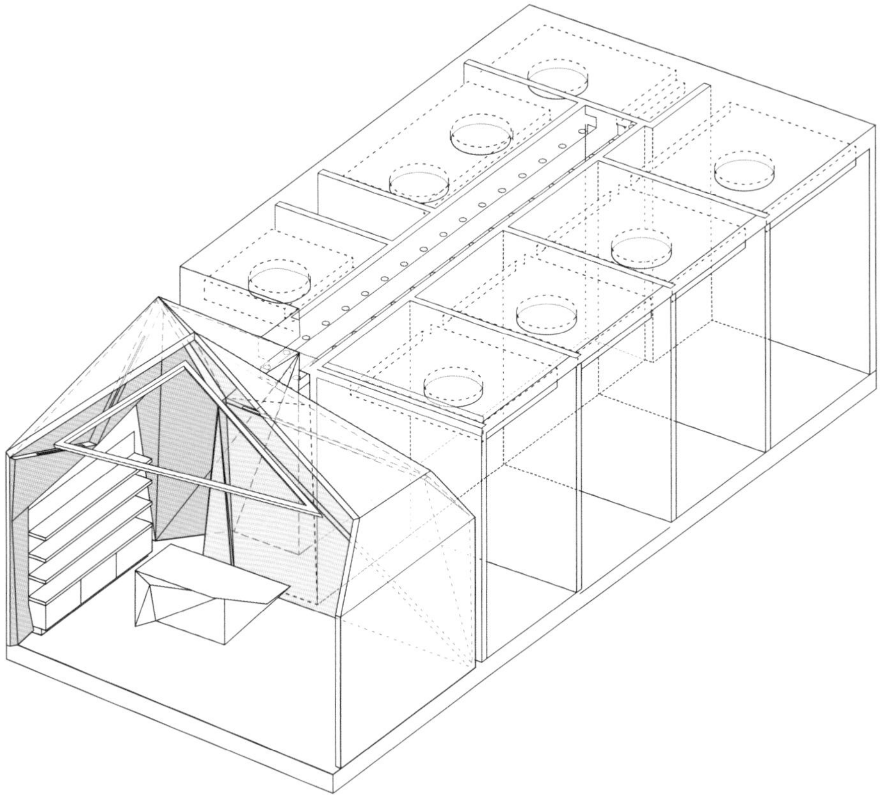

dermalogica
dermalogica
dermalogica

SHAPE HOUSE PLUS

Shape House is an urban spa that promotes the ancient wellness practice of sweating as a way to "burn calories, deepen sleep, improve skin, lift moods, and change lives." Clients sweat in darkened rooms and then cool down in a "relax room," before heading back to work or home. The founder of Shape House joined forces with the developer of a "shower spa," a place to recharge and refresh. The spa houses not just showers but makeup stations and lockers for storing evening clothes, giving people who work in the city a place to change before going out.

The site is the second floor of a landmarked building in the Flatiron District. Clients enter via the reception area and retail space, which overlook 18th Street through a full wall of windows. The spa area is accessed through the two locker rooms—in the form of curved enclosures separated by glass panels. Distinguished by the pitched roof of the Shape House logo, the largest sweat room projects from the thickened wall along the east side of the space. Showers line the west wall, with the curved volume of the relax room floating between the two zones. Sink areas and makeup stations are carved into the volumes, creating curved void spaces between the volumes. Customized Watermark Plumbing fixtures provide color accents. Cove lighting in the spa area and dimmable pendants in the sweat rooms provide soft illumination, with brighter recessed lighting inside the showers and locker rooms. Unlike the wet area floors, which are tiled, the sweating spaces and relax room are carpeted, for a gentle feel and calming acoustics.

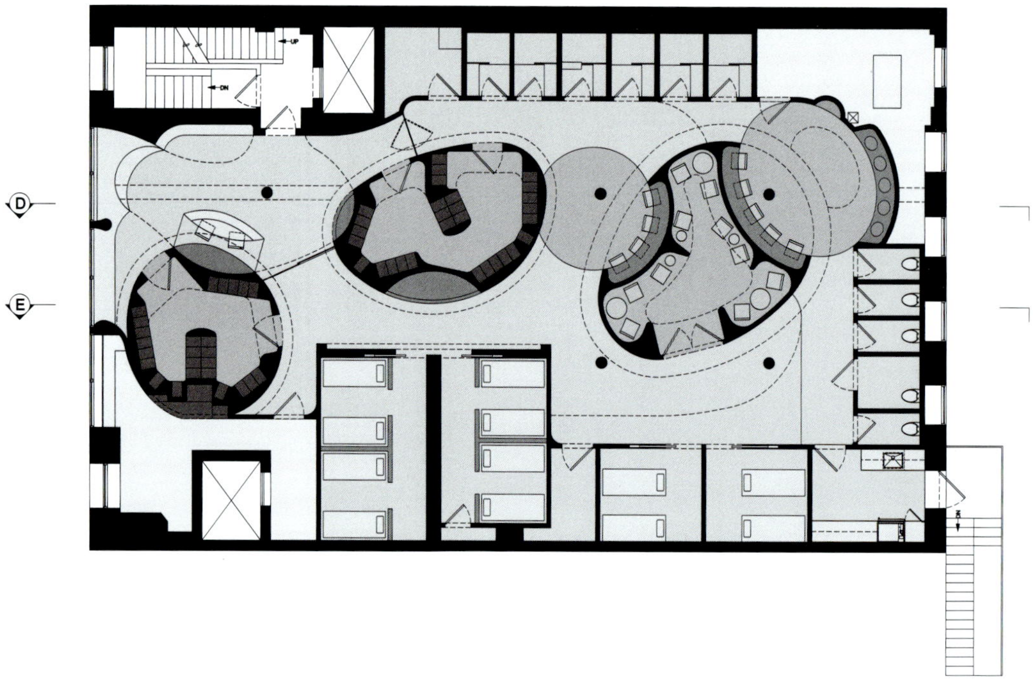
D
E

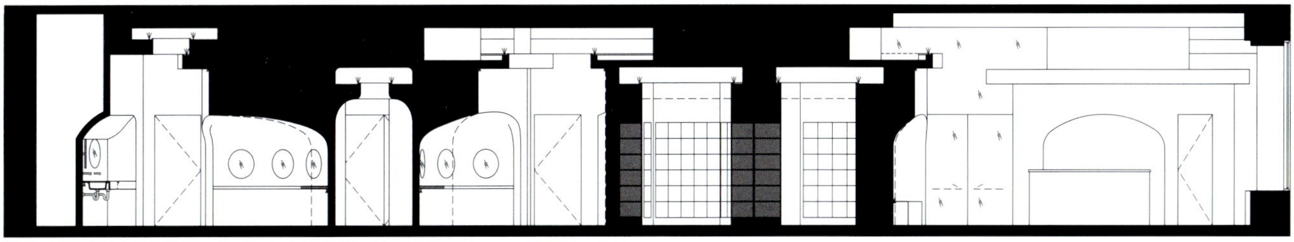

D

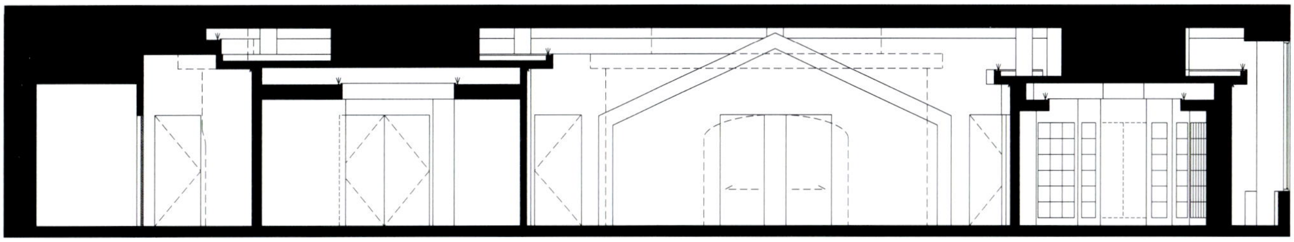

E

AFTERWORD

A number of texts about inhabitation, building circulation, and the architectural promenade have served as inspiration and sources of reference for the 25 years I have been studying and practicing architecture.

"To live is to leave traces," wrote Walter Benjamin, a German philosopher and thinker, in 1938. Benjamin's focus was surfaces in which the evidence of everyday use is imprinted. What he called the "birth of the interior" occurred in Paris during the industrial revolution in the 1800s, when mass production led to an increase in leisure time. This produced new spatial potential for inhabitation, both private and public (the latter including Paris's arcades). Benjamin saw this type of nineteenth-century inhabitation as unsuitable for the era in which he was writing. In his conversations with fellow theorist Bertolt Brecht he spoke of seeking to "erase the trace," in order to live in a space uncluttered with collected objects, memories, and history. He saw the potential of large panes of glass and steel in modern residential architecture to create spaces in which it would be difficult to leave personal imprints. Such pavilion-like houses as the 1929 Barcelona Pavilion by the German architect Ludwig Mies van der Rohe and the 1949 Glass House by the American architect Philip Johnson would seem to embody this aspiration. Ultimately, however, rather than eschewing objects and traces, these structures became jewel boxes for the few carefully curated possessions of their inhabitants. Fingerprints left their imprints on glass and steel. Traces were not erased.

In the 1970s, the theorist Robin Evans returned to the idea of the trace. He wrote about the plan as a registration of the activity of its intended occupants. "If anything is described by the architectural plan, it is the nature of human relationships, since the elements whose trace it records—walls, doors, windows and stairs—are employed first to divide and then selectively to re-unite." His essay "Figures, Doors and Passages" followed the historical development of the corridor in residential architecture, beginning in the 1500s, as a space distinct from a room. He examined the way in which the separation of circulation from spaces for habitation reflected changing ways of living.

He noted that the passages were developed in part to meet the needs for privacy and hierarchy. In particular, servants could travel down hallways without interacting with the residents and guests of a house. The rooms, however, remained enfiladed—connected by openings that aligned to create a vista available to those residents and guests.

Evans notes that an ancillary effect of the development of the hallway was to reduce the possibility for chance encounters. He describes two types of spatial conditions in the house: "architecture to look through" (rooms) versus "architecture to hide in" (corridors). The two conditions were also understood as those designed for the eye—sightlines extending the length of the interior, and possibly beyond—as opposed to those designed for movement. Later developments blurred the categories: the houses of the eighteenth-century English architect John Soane, he notes, aligned views with grand staircases and passages rather than with rooms. Still the diagram of dividing spatial conditions into the categories of trajectory and position remained.

Shifting forward to the work of the great Swiss Modernist Le Corbusier, Robert Levit analyzes the "free plan, where structure, partitions and building envelope are independent systems, as an attempt to bring the conditions of the wandering subject and the idealized order of the grid together." The figural walls and stairs of houses like the Villa Stein, built in 1927, create architectural promenades within the space. A concept originally associated with landscape architecture, the architectural promenade can be characterized by a deliberate misalignment between the physical path of movement and the established axial views within an exterior environment. In the Villa Stein, assemblies of furniture-like elements define figural paths of movement through the interior of the house. In contrast, the ribbon windows at the perimeter delineate sweeping horizontal views of the exterior.

William JR Curtis writes about the "mental maps and social landscapes" in the work of Spanish architects Enric Miralles and Carme Pinos, which he describes as exploring an ambiguous middle ground between sculpture, architecture, urbanism, and landscape. Curtis describes elements that directly relate to human use and movement, including ramps, bridges, platforms, stairs, decks, benches, steps, and railings, which are dramatized, made to hover or else interpenetrate. Promenades slide between curving, sloping walls, connecting building to site, interior to vista, mapping a "network of social relationships." He describes the work as embodying a "social landscape" in which institutions, context, and nature are cast in an interactive relationship, as in the pair's Hostalets Civic Center and Igualada Cemetery.

The combinatory aspect of elements and pathways in their work inspires the concept of assemblies.

ACKNOWLEDGMENTS

I would like to thank the many present and past members of BAAO for their incredible efforts to bring these projects to life, including Adrien Allred, Christina Ostermier, Ryan Griffin, Annie Paz, Michael Polanco, CJ Rabey, Olivia Vien, Suzanne Agbayani, Caroline Vickery, Michael Licht, Molly Hare, Megan Hurford, Ulrika Lindell, Michelle Nichols, Walter Shih, Lauren DeMattia, Ben Martinson, and Scott Savage, as well as to Priya Patel and Esther Beke of 4|MATIV for their efforts on the Maple Street School.

I extend further thanks to our expediters Phil Ferrara and Agouti Expediting; our structural engineers Zaki Albanna, Michael Barry, and Craft Engineering; our MEP engineers Bruce Merdjan and Sam Rimawi for their partnership in the technical development of our projects; and our contractors PTL Contracting, CK Construction, Altek Construction, Sandbar Contractors, Bolt Construction, Regal Renovators, John Beyer, Fowa Construction, and the Allan Group, who expertly translated our drawings into built form.

With regard to this publication, I would like to thank our photographers Francis Dzikowski and Lesley Unruh and our stylist Brice Gaillard for creating amazing images, the book's interviewer Ian Volner for organizing and thematizing our rambling conversations, and Susan Grant Lewin and Fred Bernstein for providing instrumental feedback on the texts and images.

Thank you to our clients, our design collaborators, who continue to inspire us. Our collective efforts took the work in directions that we would not have conceptualized on our own.

Great appreciation also goes to my colleagues at Pratt Institute, on whose feedback I rely, as well as to my professors at the GSD, Monica Ponce de Leon, Sheila Kennedy, Linda Pollak, and Jim Williamson, whose teaching continues to guide me. Thank you also to my former employers and mentors Toshiko Mori, Adam Yarinsky, Stephen Cassell, and Scott Cohen, who gave me valuable experience under their leadership.

And finally I'd like to thank my family, Reid, Eleanora, and Nicholas, as well as my extended family, and the families of the entire BAAO team, for their constant support.

IMAGE CREDITS

Francis Dzikowski
Cover and pp 5, 7, 9, 13–16, 20–23, 29, 31, 39–59, 61–127

Lesley Unruh
pp 2, 10–11, 18–19, 27, 128–145

BAAO Architects
pp 25, 33–35, 37, 153–159

ORO Editions
Publishers of Architecture, Art, and Design
Gordon Goff: Publisher

www.oroeditions.com
info@oroeditions.com

Published by ORO Editions

Book Design by Pablo Mandel
Managing Editor: Jake Anderson

10 9 8 7 6 5 4 3 2 1 First Edition

ISBN: 978-1-940743-90-5

Color Separations and Printing: ORO Group Ltd.
Printed in China.

ORO Editions makes a continuous effort to minimize the overall carbon footprint of its publications. As part of this goal, ORO Editions, in association with Global ReLeaf, arranges to plant trees to replace those used in the manufacturing of the paper produced for its books. Global ReLeaf is an international campaign run by American Forests, one of the world's oldest nonprofit conservation organizations. Global ReLeaf is American Forests' education and action program that helps individuals, organizations, agencies, and corporations improve the local and global environment by planting and caring for trees.